RUBANK EDUCATIONAL LIBRARY No. 39

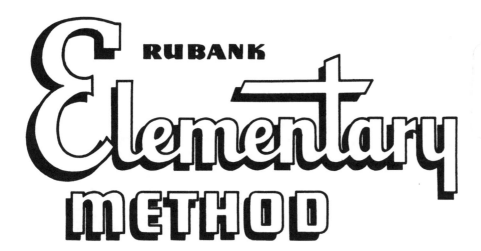

RUBANK
Elementary
METHOD

TROMBONE OR
BARITONE

NEWELL H. LONG

A FUNDAMENTAL COURSE FOR INDIVIDUAL
OR LIKE-INSTRUMENT CLASS INSTRUCTION

RUBANK®

HAL•LEONARD®
CORPORATION
7777 W. BLUEMOUND RD. P.O. BOX 13819 MILWAUKEE, WI 53213

T0071530

Chart of Slide Trombone Positions and Baritone Fingerings

The air within a trombone or baritone (or any other instrument with a cup mouthpiece) may be made to vibrate as a whole or in fractions of its length by varying the tension of the player's lips. The various pitches thus produced in each of the seven slide positions (and valve combinations) are indicated in the following table:

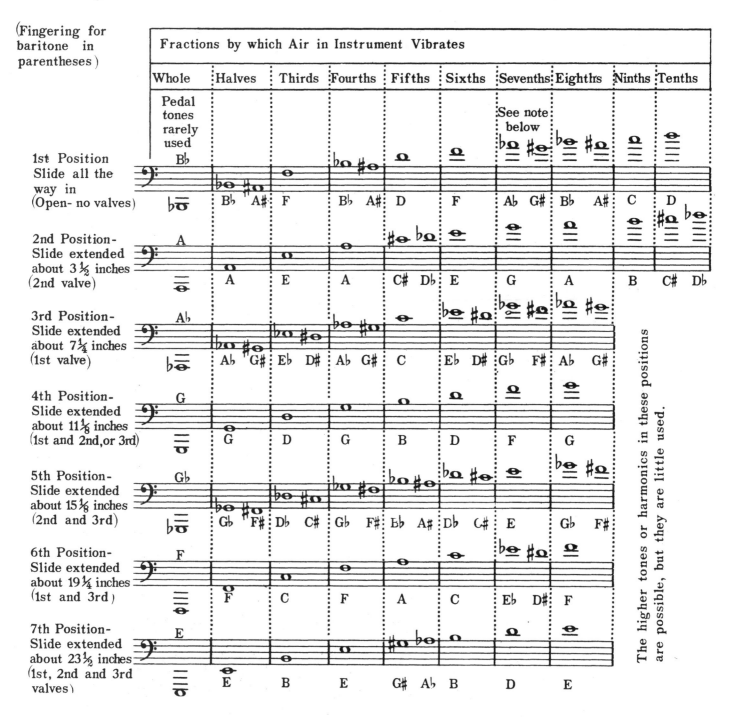

NOTE: All tones produced by the air vibrating in sevenths are flat and must be corrected by making the position for that tone about an inch shorter. This, of course, is impossible in 1st position on trombone and in all fingerings on baritone. The baritone player must chose a different fingering for the required tone or force it into tune with his lips. The latter is seldom satisfactory.

Whole Notes

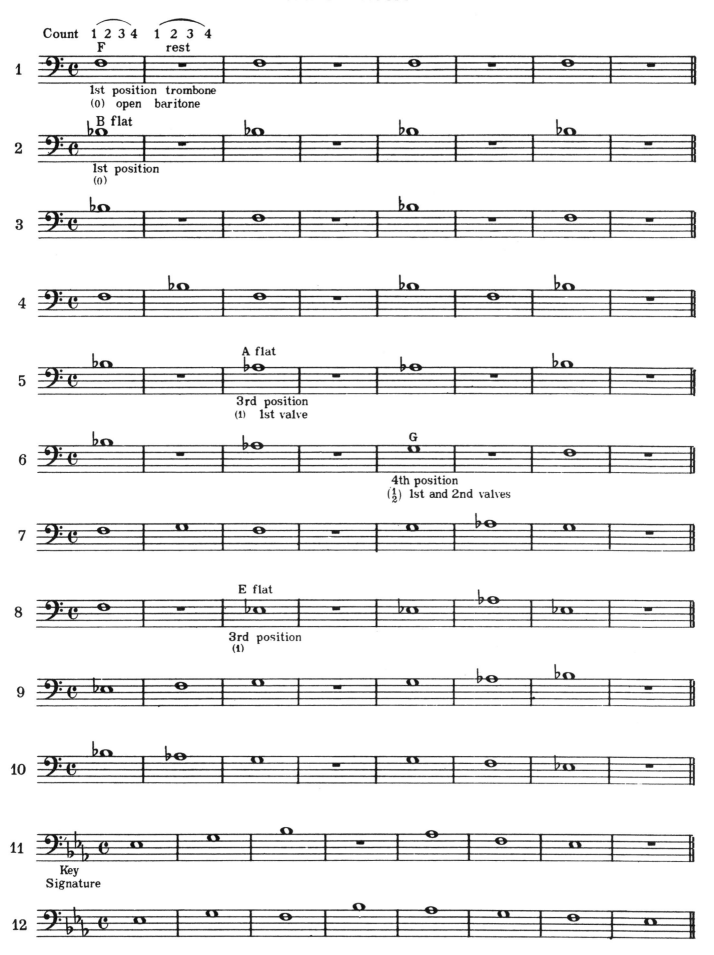

Whole Notes and Half Notes

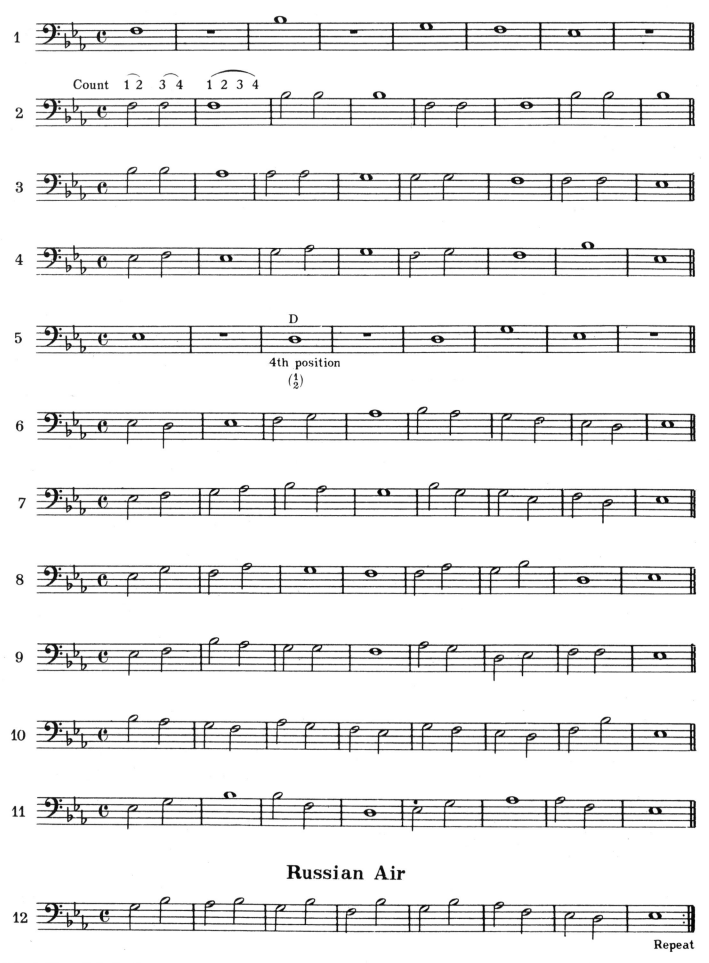

Russian Air

Repeat

Quarter Notes

Lightly Row

Folk Melody

Extending the Range - Sixth Position

Take a breath only where there is a ⸴ - comma or breathing mark.

Rubank Elem. Meth. for Trom. or Bar. 47

6

Dotted Half Notes - ¾ Measure

Hursley

Merry Widow Waltz

LEHAR

tie

play as one note

Lovely Evening

NOTE: Lovely Evening may be played as a round by two or three trombones or baritones.

Key of B-flat – Two flats

At Pierrot's Door

Ties and Accidentals

Abide With Me

Rubank Elem. Meth. for Trom. or Bar. 47

9

Eighth Notes

Long, Long Ago

²⁄₄ Measure

Hungarian Dance

Crambambuli

American Folk Song

GLUCK

Dotted Quarter and Eighth Notes

Count (a) 1 2 & 3 4 (b) 1 2 & 3 4 (c) (d) (e)

Measures (b) and (c) sound the same

Stars of the Summer Night

WOODBURY

All Through the Night

Auld Lang Syne

5
America the Beautiful

B (natural)

4th position
(½)

America

Half and Quarter Rests

Swan Song from "Lohengrin"

WAGNER

Rubank Elem. Meth. for Trom. or Bar. 47

13

Eighth Note Rhythms

German Folk Song

Reuben, Reuben

Rubank Elem. Meth. for Trom. or Bar. 47

14

Duets 1 and 2 on page 47 may be introduced at this time.

Extending Lower Range

2nd position
(2)

4th position
(1/2)

6th position
(1/3)

O No, John

English Folk Song

Chromatic Scale

Ex. 2 and Ex. 3 on this page should be played; the others are optional.

★NOTE: Effect of an "accidental" lasts throughout the measure unless cancelled by another "accidental."

ASSIGNMENT — Write the position (or fingering) under each note in Ex. 4 and 5.

More Accidentals – 5th Position

Supplementary Songs with Accidentals
and Review of Rhythms

Go Down, Moses

I Heard the Bells on Christmas Day

How Can I Leave Thee

There's Music in the Air

Eroica
Adapted from Finale of Beethoven's Third Symphony

Eighth Rest

Theme from Oberon Overture

WEBER

Night of Love Waltz

FOX

★ NOTE: Tie brings effect of the accidental into the next measure, but for the tied note only.

Key of F - One Flat

Air from "Zampa"

HEROLD

Blue Bells Of Scotland

⁶⁄₈ Measure - Six Counts to the Measure

French Pastoral Melody

Wake, O Wake from "Faust"

GOUNOD

Petite Chanson

FRENCH

Key of A flat - Four Flats

Alma Mater

College Song

Fine

D. S. al Fine

Alla Breve · (Cut Time)

C indicates **4/4** measure   **¢** indicates **2/2** measure

Polish Folk Song

If additional drill on Alla Breve is desired, review Lessons 4 and 11 playing those exercises in Alla Breve - **¢**.

Rubank Elem. Meth. for Trom. or Bar. 47   23

Key of C - No Flats or Sharps

Prayer of Thanksgiving

Netherlands Air

Silent Night

GRÜBER

⁶⁄₈ Measure - Two Counts to the Measure

Practice this lesson slowly, counting six to each measure, before trying it in two counts.

★Row, Row, Row Your Boat

★Three Blind Mice

High Barbary

Sea Chantey

Pop! Goes the Weasel

★ Note: May be played as a round by 2, 3, or 4 instruments.

Review of Five Keys and Accidentals

Practice Exercise 1 slowly (6 counts) at first; when familiar with it, try it faster (2 counts)

Practice Exercise 2 in 4 counts at first; later try the alla breve (2 counts)

A dot over a note, or under a note, means that it is to be played staccato, that is, cut the note short, releasing the tone almost as soon as it starts.

Review LESSON 17, page 21, counting two to the measure.

Rubank Elem. Meth. for Trom. or Bar. 47

26

Sixteenth Notes

Reveille

Played entirely with 4th position (valves 1 & 2)

Adjutant's Call

Theme from Symphony

HAYDN

Accent tongue more forcefully than other notes

Variation On Adeste Fideles

Dotted Eighth and Sixteenth Notes

Largo from "New World Symphony"
DVORAK

Gold Motive
WAGNER

Battle Hymn of the Republic

Lip Slurs without Slide Shifts

Increase the tension of the lips, drawing the corners of the mouth back toward the cheeks to slur to a higher tone; loosen the lips to slur to a lower tone. Tongue only the first note under each slur ⌒.

To the Colors

(Play throughout in 6th position valves 1 and 3)

Mountain Song

Celeste Aida

VERDI

Key of D-flat - Five Flats

Sweet and Low

BARNBY

Lip Slurs of Three Tones

1 "too-ee-oo"

Play this entire exercise in 4th position (Valves land 2)

"too-ee-oo-ee - ee-oo-oo"

2 6th (⅓) _____ 5th (⅔) _____ 4th (½) _____

3rd (1) _____ 2nd (2) _____ 1st (0) _____

3 5th _____

5th _____

2nd 5th 2nd   1st 5th 1st   5th _____

English May Dance

4 Fine

D. C. al Fine

Slavic Hymn

5

Lip Slurs with Slide Shifts of One Position

The Ash Grove

Welsh Melody

Lullaby

BRAHMS

Key of G - One Sharp

Love's Old Sweet Song

MOLLOY

Syncopation

(Repeat alla breve ¢)

Little 'Liza Jane

Syncopation *(continued)*

1 Three times — 1st time 4/4; 2nd and 3rd times ¢; MEMORIZE

Bohemian Dance

Lively

2

The Old Ark's A-Moverin'

Negro Spiritual

Moderato

4 This may be tried in ¢ after thoroughly learned in moderate 4/4

3 Three times — 1st time 4/4; 2nd and 3rd times ¢; MEMORIZE

Joshua Fit De Battle of Jericho

Negro Spiritual

Slow — Fast★

5

Fine.

cresc.

Lip slur

D. C. al Fine

★ Work this out at a slow tempo, counting the time carefully, before trying it at a rapid tempo.

Four Characteristic Studies

May be used as tests

Three Minor Keys

D Minor

Harmonic Minor Scale

Melodic Minor Scale

B-flat Minor

F Minor

Song of the Volga Boatmen

Russian

Slowly

Legato Playing

In preceding lessons the slur mark ⌒ has been used only to indicate lip slurs. It has however, a more general meaning and when it appears over a group of notes it signifies that these notes are to be played as a musical unit or phrase and that the tone of the instrument in passing from one note to another will be as smooth as possible. The same meaning is expressed by the word <u>legato</u> written at the beginning of a melody or phrase.

To play <u>legato</u> on most wind instruments it is merely necessary to tongue the first note under the slur and sustain the tone while passing from one note to the next without additional tongue attacks. The flow of air through the instrument is uninterrupted during the slur. If this procedure were followed for the slide trombone, glissandos ("smears") would be produced between tones on the same harmonic (See Position Chart. page 2) To avoid these "smears" and acquire a legato style of trombone playing the following rules should be observed.

1. Use a <u>soft tongue attack</u>. Instead of using the rather explosive "too", attack with a light "doo" syllable.

2. <u>Shift the slide quickly</u> between notes and make the interruption in tone while the slide is being shifted as slight as possible. Recontinue the tone after the shift with a very light "doo" attack.

3. When two notes of different pitches are connected by a slur and can be played with the same slide position, the <u>lip slur</u> should be used if the player can use it smoothly.

4. The lip slur should also be used when the slide shifts just one position, in or out, and the tone skips up or down more than a half step (semitone).

Examples of skips effective as lip slurs

2nd   2nd   4th   4th   3rd   2nd   4th   5th   2nd   1st   3rd   4th

5. Sometimes it is possible to lip slur a skip when the slide moves two positions in or out provided that, if the slide moves out, the change is to a higher tone, and if the slide moves in, the change is to a lower tone.

Examples

2nd   4th   1st   3rd   3rd   1st   4th   2nd

6. By being familiar with the different positions in which the same note may be played (See Chart, page 2) the player can choose less common positions for some of the notes in order that lip slurs may be introduced to improve the legato playing.

"doo   doo   doo"   lip slur.   "doo   doo   doo"   lip slur.

1st   4th   1st   4th   4th   1st   4th   4th   5th   4th

Legato Playing

(Notes to be connected by lip slurs are marked ⌐¬. Those which may be connected by the more difficult lip slurs explained in Rule 5 on the preceding page are marked ......)

Swanee River
FOSTER

In the Gloaming
HARRISON

Santa Lucia
Italian

Theme from "Pathetic Symphony"
Tschaikowsky

Triplets

Old Welsh Hymn

Theme from "Lohengrin"

WAGNER

Theme from Fourth Symphony

SCHUMANN

Triplets Abreviated   May be written

★ Note: The two notes should be played with the slide positions shortened about an inch to bring them in tune.

$\frac{12}{8}$ and $\frac{9}{8}$ Measures

Andante Cantabile From Fifth Symphony

TSCHAIKOWSKY

Air from "Faust"

GOUNOD

Theme from Ride of the Walkyries

WAGNER

Rapid Tongue Attack

Abreviations used in this lesson:

Broken Chords and Lip Slurs

A "Warming-up" Lip Slur Exercise

Repeat in
these positions
5th 4th 3rd 2nd 1st
(²⁄₃) (½) (1) (2) (0)

Study in Lip Slurs

Slowly

D. C. al Fine

Four Notes to One Count

Arkansas Traveler

Complex Rhythms

High Notes - Clefs

The five examples at the right show how the same phrase looks when written in five different clefs. All five sound and are played the same.

Notice the differences in key signatures and "accidentals."

How many lines and spaces higher or lower than bass clef is each of the others written?

See if you can figure out a method of your own for reading each one of these clefs.

BASS CLEF - The usual trombone clef.

TREBLE CLEF - CONCERT KEY - Knowledge of this clef useful for playing from vocal music.

TREBLE CLEF TRANSPOSED for B♭ instrument. Much used by baritonists; formerly by trombonists.

TENOR CLEF - Used in symphony orchestra trombone parts and in some European band editions.

ALTO CLEF - Once used for 1st trombone parts in symphony orchestra music; no longer so used.

DUETS

For 2 Trombones, 2 Baritones, or Trombone and Baritone

Polish Folk Song

My Faith Looks Up to Thee

Old Black Joe

Nobody Knows the Trouble I've Seen

Wearing of the Green

German Waltz

Drink To Me Only With Thine Eyes

D.C. al Fine

Integer Vitae

Scandinavian Dance

Two Part Invention

QUARTETS
Ode from "Pirates of Penzance"

SULLIVAN

Choral

BACH

Stars of the Summer Night

WOODBURY

Trombone Quartet from "Pathetic Symphony"

TSCHAIKOWSKY

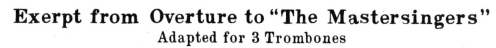

Exerpt from Overture to "The Mastersingers"
Adapted for 3 Trombones

WAGNER

Rubank Elem. Meth. for Trom. or Bar. 47

52